CHAMPIONSHIPS WON — ATLANTA HAWKS

1

1958 – 4 games to 2 vs. Boston Celtics

HAWKS
14

NBA CHAMPIONS

ATLANTA HAWKS

BY MICHAEL E. GOODMAN

CREATIVE EDUCATION CREATIVE PAPERBACKS

Al Horford had his best season for the Hawks in 2013–14.

18.6
points per game (average)

33.1
minutes per game (average)

34
career-high points in a game (2/27/13; 12/13/13)

On the cover – Dennis Schröder

TABLE OF CONTENTS

DOMINIQUE WILKINS / BOB HAGAN / JOHN DREW / JOE J SMITH / EDDIE JOHNSON /

Published by Creative Education and Creative Paperbacks

P.O. Box 227, Mankato, Minnesota 56002

Creative Education and Creative Paperbacks are imprints of The Creative Company

www.thecreativecompany.us

Design and production by Blue Design

Art direction by Rita Marshall

Printed in the United States of America

Photographs by AP Images (Associated Press), Corbis (Andrew Snook/Icon SMI), Getty Images (Andrew D. Bernstein/NBAE, Bettmann, Kevin C. Cox/Getty Images Sport, Gary G. Dineen/Sporting News, Focus on Sport, Jesse D. Garrabrant/NBAE, Noah Graham/NBAE, Thearon W. Henderson/Getty Images Sport, Walter Iooss Jr./NBAE, Walter Iooss Jr./Sports Illustrated, Ken Levine/Allsport, George Long/WireImage, Richard Meek/Sports Illustrated, Maddie Meyer/Getty Images Sport, Jason Miller, Doug Pensinger/Getty Images Sport, Rogers Photo Archive, Don Allen Sparks)

Library of Congress Cataloging-in-Publication Data

Names: Goodman, Michael E., author.

Title: Atlanta Hawks / Michael E. Goodman.

Series: NBA Champions.

Includes index.

Summary: Jump into the NBA action with this high-interest account of the Atlanta Hawks pro basketball team, including league championships won and star players such as Dominique Wilkins.

Identifiers: LCCN 2017035448 / ISBN 978-1-64026-013-9 (hardcover) / ISBN 978-1-62832-568-3 (pbk) / ISBN 978-1-64000-042-1 (eBook)

Subjects: LCSH: 1. Atlanta Hawks (Basketball team)—History—Juvenile literature. 2. Atlanta Hawks (Basketball team)—Biography—Juvenile literature.

Classification: LCC GV885.52.A7 G66 2018 / DDC 796.323/6409758231—dc23

CCSS: RI.1.1, 2, 3, 4, 5, 6, 7; RI.2.1, 2, 5, 6; RI.3.1, 5; RI.4.3, 5; RF.1.1, 3, 4; RF.2.3, 4

First Edition HC 9 8 7 6 5 4 3 2 1

First Edition PBK 9 8 7 6 5 4 3 2 1

/ LENNY WILK BLAYLOCK / DA PETE MARAVIC / JEFF TEAGUE / MARVIN WILL BELLAMY / PAU

/ ALAN HENDERSON / DENN SHAREEF ABDUR-RAHIM / RIC

TTIT / LOU HUDSON / CLIFF
NSON / KEVIN WILLIS / JOSH
LMO BEATY / BILL BRIDGES
S / AL HORFORD / MOOKIE
ROUNDFIELD / DOC RIVERS /
JASON TERRY / STEVE SMITH
OE CALDWELL / TREE ROLLINS
MS / STACEY AUGMON / WALT
MILLSAP / CLYDE LOVELLETTE
SCHRÖDER / STEVE HAWES /
GUERIN / CLIFF LEVINGSTON

ATLANTA IS HOME TO PRO TEAMS IN BASEBALL, FOOTBALL, BASKETBALL, AND SOCCER.

HOME OF THE HAWKS

Atlanta is the largest city in Georgia. Atlanta began as a small town near a train line. Now it has the world's busiest airport. Atlanta has an **arena** called Philips Arena. It is the home of a basketball team called the Hawks.

How the Hawks Got Their Name

In 1832, an Indian chief named Black Hawk led a war against the United States Army. It was fought near three cities in Illinois and Iowa. A new basketball team, the Tri-Cities Blackhawks, formed in the area in 1946. When the team moved to Milwaukee, its name was shortened to Hawks.

HOT RIVALS

The Hawks are part of the National Basketball Association (NBA). They play against other teams in the NBA. They try to win the **NBA Finals**. The Hawks' main **rivals** are the Heat, Hornets, Magic, and Wizards.

1958 FINALS

1958 NBA FINALS — HAWKS VS. CELTICS (HAWKS WON 4–2)

BOB PETTIT SCORED 50 POINTS AND GRABBED 19 REBOUNDS IN GAME 6.

THIS WAS A REMATCH OF THE TWO TEAMS FROM THE YEAR BEFORE.

THE HAWKS WON EACH OF THEIR GAMES BY THREE POINTS OR FEWER.

THIS WAS THE LAST TIME THE HAWKS WON THE FINALS.

IN THEIR NINTH YEAR AS A TEAM, THE HAWKS HAD ALREADY CHANGED HOMETOWNS TWICE.

PETTIT AND CLIFF HAGAN SCORED 63 OF ATLANTA'S 104 POINTS IN GAME 1.

OHIO NATIVE DON OTTEN PLAYED FOR THE HAWKS UNTIL 1950.

THE BLACKHAWKS

The Hawks started playing in 1946 in the Midwest. They were called the Tri-Cities Blackhawks. Their best player was high-scoring center Don Otten. In 1951, they moved to Milwaukee, Wisconsin.

In 1954, the Hawks **drafted** college star Bob Pettit. The forward/center soon became the team's top scorer and **rebounder**. The next year, Pettit and the Hawks moved to St. Louis, Missouri.

BOB PETTIT — 1959 NBA MVP

Bob Pettit always tried to improve his game. After being named Rookie of the Year in 1955, he became the NBA's first MVP in 1956. He led the Hawks to the NBA title in 1958. The following year, he earned MVP honors a second time. His 29.2 points per game average was a league record at the time.

Cliff Hagan

Jack Coleman

Joe Johnson

Cliff Hagan had 9 playoff appearances in his 10 Hawks seasons.

Julius Erving

Dominique Wilkins

Kyle Korver

In 2015, the Hawks had their best season ever, going 60-22.

Bob Pettit

Coach Mike Fratello

Josh Smith

Al Horford

Alexander Volkov

BECOMING CHAMPIONS

Fans in St. Louis cheered loudest for Pettit and forward Cliff Hagan. They led the team to the NBA Finals in 1957 and 1958. The Hawks almost won the first year. Then, in 1958, they became world champions!

The Hawks have not been in the Finals since 1961.

Dennis Schröder and Coach Budenholzer

Jeff Teague

Tree Rollins

In 1968, the Hawks moved to Atlanta. Their star center Wayne Rollins was tall and strong. So people called him "Tree." The Atlanta Hawks reached the **playoffs** many times. But they could not win another championship.

NUMBER OF SEASONS IN THE PLAYOFFS — ATLANTA HAWKS

THE HAWKS HAVE BEEN IN THE PLAYOFFS

46

TIMES FROM 1949 THROUGH 2017.

FORWARD PAUL MILLSAP HELPED THE HAWKS REACH THE PLAYOFFS FROM 2013 TO 2017.

Spud Webb
played 12 years for 4 teams.

4,342
career assists

8,072
career points

The Hawks have made the playoffs 46 times.*

4	1
in Finals	NBA title

* As of 2017–18

STARS OF THE HAWKS

Several Hawks leaders were short and quick. Guard Slater Martin was a fine passer for the 1958 champs. Tiny Spud Webb ran the team from 1985 to 1991.

During the 1970s, **swingman** Lou Hudson was a great jump shooter. His number 23 jersey now hangs in Philips Arena. Dominique Wilkins's number 21 jersey hangs there, too. His highflying dunks amazed fans during the 1980s and 1990s.

The Hawks traded for forward Paul Millsap in 2013. He was named to the **All-Star team** four years in a row. When he left in 2017, Atlanta fans hoped a new star would help their club become champions again.

Lou Hudson played 730 games over 11 seasons.

16,049 points

2,098 assists

ABOUT THE HAWKS

STARTED PLAYING: 1946
CONFERENCE/DIVISION: EASTERN CONFERENCE, SOUTHEAST DIVISION
TEAM COLORS: RED, BRIGHT GREEN, AND GRAY

GLOSSARY

ALL-STAR TEAM—a special team made up of the best players in each NBA conference

ARENA—a large building for indoor sports events; it has many seats for fans

DRAFTED—chosen by a team from the best players in college or other countries

NBA FINALS—a series of games between two teams at the end of the playoffs; the first team to win four games is the champion

PLAYOFFS—games played after the regular season by the best teams to see who the champion will be

REBOUNDER—a player who catches and controls the ball after a missed shot

RIVALS—teams that play extra hard against each other

SWINGMAN—a basketball player who can play guard or forward

INDEX

NBA website for kids: http://jr.nba.com/